Nature

A Poetry Collection

MARIO PANAYI

Dedication

In alphabetical order, dedicated to Clover, Jeremy, Michelle, and Sir David (four exceptional but very different individuals).

Clover is the Labrador on the cover of this book. Never met you but I know you bring much joy to your owner and that you are spoiled with adventures, holidays and walks. Despite being spoiled, your character and personality remains unspoilt with genuine happiness, empathy and a good nature.

Jeremy Jeavons supplied one of the photos for the cover of this book. He enjoys walking, observing nature and even conquered the three peaks challenge. He also supplied a photo for a previous book (*What flower, bush or tree are YOU?*) – au naturel with a shocked face and just fig leaves covering his shame.

Michelle Emerson is my dedicated editor and publisher who also loves walking and observing nature. Michelle is prompt, hardworking and produces the most magnificent of books. Her editing and publishing services can be found at www.michelleemerson.co.uk.

Move over Mother Nature; the real Father of Nature is Sir David Attenborough. He is, without doubt, the undisputed king of nature and the natural world, having educated, inspired and informed audiences for several decades.

Contents

Air

You are free-flowing
Crisp, fresh and essential
But like with most innocent things
Others will cruelly take advantage
Ravenously and without remorse
They'll absorb your essence
Polluting and damaging your existence

Avalanche

You are cold and deadly
Your attack is sudden
Spontaneously becoming dangerous
Rapidly gathering speed
Unsurmountable power
Leaving no survivors
In fact you're so lethal
That you even try
To bury all the evidence

Balanced Diet

From the age of dinosaurs
Until the modern world
There have been carnivores
Herbivores and omnivores
Vegans, vegetarians and meat-eaters
Fruitarians and pescatarians
Some have evolved to survive
Others, it is a lifestyle choice
And it goes to show
That whether wild or domesticated
Whether small and tiny or large and humungous
What we eat is not defined specifically by our species
That the different animals that exist
Have similarities well beyond the physical attributes

Beach Sand

So many people like to visit you
You are fine and smooth
You are an example
Of no matter what your age
You can still be beautiful
Attracting both young and old
You are so resilient
For no matter what pranks
Children do with their bucket and spades
You just let it all wash over you
Like salty sea water rippling over sand

Biodiversity

Biodiversity is the scientific measure
Of the variety of species, habitats and ecosystems
In other words the variety of fauna and flora
Meaning the variety of animals and plants
A rainforest with thousands of different types of trees
Will be a home to thousands and thousands of animals
Hence that rainforest will be rich in biodiversity
A piece of land that flourishes in only one tree type
Will be very low in biodiversity as few species will live
  there
There is a co-dependence of animals and plants
So if there is an extinction or reduction in flora
That will affect the variety of fauna and vice versa
The biggest threat by far to biodiversity
Is the greed and thirst of humans

Birth

It is both wonderful and painful
Something that all animals have in common
All women across all lands
Various species in oceans and forests

Yet despite the shared experiences
The desperate natural struggles for survival
It is unnatural phenomena such as wars and disease
That threatens the lives of mothers and their babies

Cave

You are coarse and rugged
No smoothness or polished edges
Absent of any refinement
Just rough and jagged and wrinkled
Crevices here and there

Yet your appearance
Is an example that you should not judge
As you welcome anyone and everyone
Becoming a shelter to those in need
Showcasing your homely and caring nature

Climate Change

It is the long-term changes and patterns
In the world's temperature and weather
The burning of fossil fuels
Which includes coal and oil and gas
Cutting down trees in forests and jungles
The greed of mankind and corporations
Yet what is the point of such wealth
If droughts, rising sea levels, intense storms
The flooding of polar ice and aggressive wildfires
Are actually killing off your customers?

The earth is slowly choking
Becoming a chronic asthma-polluted planet
We might still have a future
But for the next generation
Their time on this dying earth
Might be limited
With a drastically reduced quality of life
A fractured lifespan
Echoing an earth on life-support

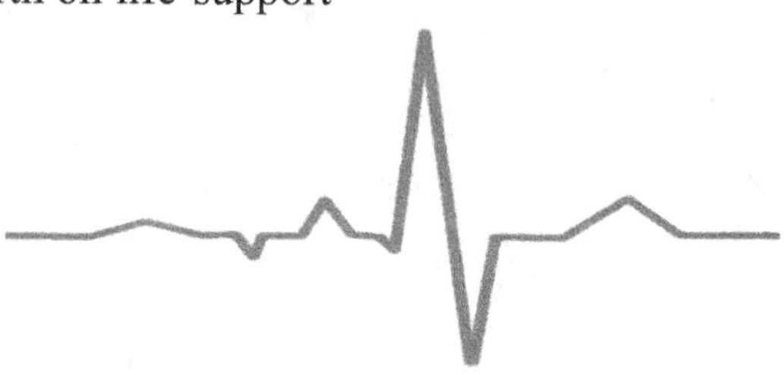

Clouds

Giant soft cotton buds
To dive into like a bouncy castle
Or sinking into heaven's cushions
Made of multiple moulted angel feathers

Oh how naïve people can be
As angelic white clouds
Can become a moody shade of grey
Before unleashing temperamental tears galore

Creek

Narrow stretch of water
Slow flowing
A build-up of sediments

Almost like a canoeist
Having lost their paddle
Hence, up the creek without a paddle

You're caught in a rut
Too many things to do
Too many thoughts clouding your judgment

Don't you realise
You're beautiful inside and out
You don't need a paddle to manoeuvre through that creek

Deserts

You are virtually barren
So dry and harsh
That animals and plants
Would struggle to survive

Yet there are a few species
That have adapted and survived
An example of determination
And of course survival of the fittest

Whilst most would think
Of dry and hot conditions
The Sahara Desert coming to mind
They forget that the polar opposite exists

There are polar deserts
Where the land is snow and ice
So are deserts natural lands where flora and fauna
Exist with minimal impact from humans?

Desserts

You are so sweet
Tender and mouth-watering
Delicious and decadent
Smooth and soft
And ……
          No

No. NO. NO.

You're in the wrong book

Drought

A period of drier-than-normal weather
That can last days, months and even years
Resulting in environmental consequences such as wildfires
In economic consequences including water supplies
And social repercussions such as excessive heat and higher
   food costs

Think about your face
Not splashing water on it
Not having a shower or bath
For days and days no water whatsoever on your skin
Letting it dehydrate and become crusty

Land suffers during droughts
Dry and barren and dying
Just like your body if you didn't drink
Your throat becoming dry
Organs slowly malfunctioning

Water is essential
For animals and humans and land
It's a slow effect
But no water
Is murder

Earthquake

You are intense
Rumbling and of seismic proportions
Making the earth itself tremble

Nothing and no one is safe
You are unrelenting
In your wave of destruction

Not content with settling down
You continue with aftershocks
Causing all to quake in your presence

Evolution

Whether man or woman
Or even plant or animal
You evolve to survive
Adapting and changing
Your body virtually metamorphosing

As environments change
So will you
It's evolve or die
Learning new skills
Developing new physiques

As the generations and eons pass along
Nature will alter in order to prosper
Human beings become stronger
But then nurture, greed and contemplation
Will interfere and influence

Natural evolution becomes tainted
By the wars of different ideals
Where good, bad and indifference battle
And so evolution itself springs
Into different directions

Extinction

Dodo Bird: *They spread false rumours that it was because I was naïve.*

Rocky Mountain Locust: *They're probably glad I'm extinct as the Bible stories about plagues of locusts made me into the ultimate villain of mankind.*

Golden Toad: *I was more orange than golden. But who really cares now that I'm extinct? p.s. Climate change contributed to my extinction. p.p.s. I almost made it to the 1990s. Almost, ☹.*

Steller's Sea Cow: *Even giants of the sea can be made extinct due to humans hunting us for our fur and oil. The Bastards.*

Labrador Duck: *Bet you've never even heard of me. I was beautiful to look at. Humans most definitely contributed to my extinction. Quack. Quack.*

Thylacine: *I know my lifespan was only 13 years old. I know they nicknamed me The Tasmanian Wolf and The Tasmanian Tiger. I thought giving me a nickname was a form of endearment and that I'd be safe. It's not even a hundred years since I was made extinct. But most of you have never heard of me and will never know what I looked like.*

Fire

It was a gift from a Titan
Flaring flames which gave warmth
Echoing the heat of lust and desire
But just like how excitement and infatuation
Can easily flare out of control
So can fires across the lands
Powerful and unrelenting
Scorching and burning
Reducing everything in its path
To dust and ash and even splinters of bone

Flowers

Naturally occurring
Beautiful scenery
With amazing fragrances

Cut down by entrepreneurs
Mass production
New species created

Bottled perfumes and shower gels
Given as gifts to put in vases
And wreaths for final farewells

The bees reducing in numbers
As they search for the fresh ones
Concrete replacing fields of flowers

Flowers

(variant version)

The bulb grows until ready
To break through the earth
Growing into an amazing
And beautiful flower

The flower is mesmerising
To all who see and the scent
Is an intoxicating and alluring fragrance
Sexily and magnetically drawing you in

Cruel harsh hands slice
Taking the flower away
From familiarity
From her natural surroundings

Forced tightly into becoming another victim
Drenched with shame below
Her beauty tainted and withering
Until dying prematurely and discarded

Fog

You are thick and dense
A cloud of grey cotton
Making vision and clarity
Virtually impossible

You are there in the morning
You are there late at night
A hangover from hell
A migraine of haziness

As though the methane
From a herd of cows and bulls
Has amassed into a floating uneven ball
That blurs what you want to see

Along with the fog
Comes the coldness of winter
A reminder of the unknown
And a reminder of mortality

Footprints

From the tiny pitter-patter footprints of ants
To the footprints of gigantic elephants
None have more of an impact upon the earth
Than the footprints of humans
Their footprints are unnatural
Not an imprint of their natural-skinned foot
But their footprint in comfy shoes and socks and slippers
Often made from the skin and bi-product of other animals
Killed and slaughtered for fashionable shoes and
    accessories
An honourable mention to the carbon footprints humans
    cause
Upon the earth and the air and even the atmosphere above
    the earth
Not forgetting the oceans and mountains and valleys
Final mention to the human footprints that trample
On work colleagues, clients, neighbours and relatives
And of course a single footprint hammering down on eight-
    legged spiders

Fossil

You are ancient
A remnant of the past
A reminder of mortality
Brittle and fragile to touch
A shell of your former life
Virtually an imprint
Of a once vibrant life

Fossils

Nothing lives forever
You live and then you die
That's if you're lucky
And over time
All that might remain
Is fossilised traces
Of your existence
Bones and shells
Exoskeletons and even imprints
Piecing together
The fragments of evolution
Your life's loves and works
Are insignificant
You are not even a memory
Just a splinter within
A world full of species
Whose lifespans are
But a blink of an eye

Fruit

Life is varied
It can be acidic and bitter
Or sweet and juicy and fresh
It can even be rotten

Life is short
Beautiful when in your prime
Smooth to touch and caress
Tasting heavenly delights

Ripeness of spring and summer
Soon turns to Autumn
As silky and sleek skin transforms
Now broken with ripples galore

The winter of death is soon upon us
Shrivelled and drooping
Soft and squishy
Dribbling daily until no more

Gas

In your natural form
You are odourless
Silent

Yet your kind
Can also be a killer
Blending in as useful

You are like everything else
Scents added, but in your case
Too much has made you smell

You are no longer
Silent as still air
You can now be detected

Surprisingly
You are still
Highly sought after

Although still in abundance
You've become expensive
Having also excelled at marketing

Glacier

You are beyond cold
A block of slippery ice
Beautiful to look at
But you are murderous
Sliding over anything natural
Ensuring their survival is brutal
Yet as with everything
Cracks will soon develop
Like the strain of a polar bear
On a sheet of ice
You can be broken
It might take years
But eventually
You will thaw

Granite

You are known for being coarse
Strong as any rock
But even the toughest
Can eventually crumble

Gravity

I don't know how you do it
But you are truly amazing
Always keeping me grounded

Ice

There are some things
That are beautiful to look at
But get too close, and you might regret it
It's like falling through ice that shatters

There are some people
That you are attracted to
But get too close, and you'll discover the real person
Either warm and attentive or cold and dangerous as ice

Iceberg

You are an example
Of a giant with hidden depth
Cold and unrelenting and on the move
Quietly destroying anything in your way

Yet giants like mortals do not live forever
Your strength and determination
Will begin to diminish
Stature slowly melting away

Whilst you are arctic and frigid
Other giants have the heat of the sun
The saltiness of oceans
Who will brutally attack you

Your legacy will of course live on
Your kind will thrive and die and thrive again
Slowly drifting with weight and presence
Always bubbling just above the surface

Jungle

Fertile land that is pure and sterile from human hands
Allowed to flourish as nature intended
A remnant of Gaea's unpolluted earth
Where animals and vegetation live
Not necessarily in harmony
As predator and prey exist
It's a haven for a natural world
No steel or plastic or fumes to taint
Lungs and hearts beating as intended

Territory of the workplace
Where laws intended for a civil society
To create a just and equal environment are ignored
Purposely wrongly interpreted and manipulated
Where the rich get richer on the hard work of others
Evolution of industry becoming convoluted
A tangled mass of intrigue, deception and skulduggery
Densely populated as the trees in a jungle
With predators feasting on the prey struggling to survive

Lakes

You are mellow
Static and stable
Tranquil and relaxing
Transporting those moods
To all who see you

You are not shallow
On the contrary
There is real depth
To reach such calmness
Almost unique

Lapland

A land where the fantasy of Christmas
Can become a reality for children
Excitement and astonishment

Where the cold and snow becomes accepted
As part of the dream of Santa Claus
Along with reindeers and tall conifer trees

A magical experience of what nature has to offer
Beautiful scenery of wildlife and landscapes
Merged with the fantasy of a not-so-secret grotto with
    presents galore

Marble

In your original state
You are marvellous to look at
Truly astonishing and all natural
But as with most things in life
We are not content with the natural look
Chiselled away and polished
Virtually changing your chemical composition
So much money and work
Finally unveiled
Slick, strong and statuesque

Meteorite

You are solid and determined
Breaking away and travelling
Getting hotter until a shooting star
Blazing bright in your boldness

Your impact upon this earth
Is significant and magnificent
Unique and eventful
A permanent specimen for all to see

You can be bright and colourful
Dull as grey and brown colours
Light or heavy, small or large
But always intriguing and mysterious

You can be smooth as glass
Or rough as rocks
Holding secrets of the galaxy
Teasing but a mere fragment of those universal secrets

Monsoon

It is summer
The weather is hot
Oh so very hot
Almost unbearable

Then an unexpected downpour
As though an ocean from above
Is emptying completely
So intense and immediate
Flooding everything

The sun so extremely hot
Has showered today
A shower of extreme proportions
In order to be able to refresh
The scorching flames of the sun

Moon

You are a star
The brightest and the biggest
All the other millions of other stars
Are almost insignificant next to you

You are instantly recognisable
Throughout the world
Shining so bright
That you bring light into the dark

Yet there are times
When you do not appear to be whole
That a piece of you is missing
Despite continuing to shine magnificently

Expectations of you are so HUGE
That you appear to be whole again
Before once more diminishing
A truly agonising bipolar existence

Mother Nature

She is beautiful
Enduring and patient
Dazzling beneath the sunlight
Her former lover Helios
Warming up her body
Basking it with the warmth of his hands
Admiring her from his home in the sun

Another former lover watches
Chained for an eternity
Trembling with anger
Body twitching
Each twitch resulting in lighting
Electrifying, loud and frightening
His eyes begin to flicker
Unable to contain his tears of sorrow
They begin to escape
Tiny tears of a God
Which results in thunderstorms upon the earth

Tartarus also reacts
Jealous and angry
How dare Gaea love others?
He unleashes with fury
Mudslides that destroy and kill
Quicksands and swamps
Anything at his disposal

Pontus reminds Mother Earth of his powers
Oceans that burn with fury

Rushing like angry ichor
Tsunami and water whirls
Washing over her earth
A tempestuous affair
As his water refreshes her dryness
Musky sea-salt fragrances
Awakening and stimulating a Goddess

The list of Mother Earth's lovers continues
Each reminding her of what they once had
But she merely continues to flourish
Her mountains remain firm
Sturdy and amazing
Her flowers awaken every spring
Along with trees that flourish
Streams flow calmly

She has tired of Gods
They are no longer her lovers
Instead it is humans that stimulate her
Their feet tickling her earth
They appreciate the scent of her
In valleys and mountains
Near ponds and rivers
They are unaware that she does actually exist

Yet she will tire of humans eventually
Selfish creatures that attack her
Cutting down her forests
Digging into her body
Extracting her natural elements
Then like Gods who used to metamorphose

The humans transform the elements
Into harmful and toxic pollution
Poisoning her and themselves

Yes Mother Earth is beautiful
Amazing and enduring
But she is being weakened
By former lovers
By her descendants
And as for her patience
Well as the cliché says
Nothing lasts forever

Mountain

You are magnificent
Ancient and full of history
Humans are drawn to you
To the danger that you possess
Looking all innocent and natural
Rough edges and crevices
On your crust-ridden exterior
With clumps of moss and dew

You are a survivor
Crisp, fresh and cold air surrounding you
Like a heavenly aura
Created from the flapping wings of angels
Yet despite your pleasant demeanour
Through no desire or intent
Not all who visit you
Are able to survive the experience

Mudslide

Initially you look reliable
Strong, sturdy and in the background
But you are so dangerous
Often without warning
You viciously attack
Speed is your power
Your charge is heavy
Obliterating anything and everyone
An avalanche of death and destruction
Then masterfully
You try to bury the evidence
Resulting in your character's nature
Being perilously slippery

Museums of Natural History and Nature

Enter the museums of natural history and nature
See in awe the genuine and authentic
Whilst all snug in clothes and shoes
Made of synthetic materials and animal produce

Enter the museums of natural history and nature
Pay with your credit cards or with notes and coins
All made from modern materials
Natural materials blended into unnatural plastic and paper

Enter the museums of natural history and nature
Walk on wooden or tiled floors
Or even on concrete whilst breathing in fresh air
The entire experience being all natural

There is much to learn in these museums
But if you are going to go for the whole experience
Would you walk barefoot like prehistoric ancestors?
And would that be a small, medium or large loin cloth you
    require?

Natural Food

What would you term as natural food?
Nuts and seeds, fresh and dried fruit?
Herbs and spices?
What about honey?
Food without preservatives?
Vegetables, eggs, fish, meat?
Especially if organic

In law what identifies natural foods?
No food additives such as hormones
No antibiotics, preservatives, sweeteners
Or food flavourings
Food that is not processed and manufactured

Perhaps the only natural food
From an ethical and moral point of view
Is purely organic and maybe even home-grown
At least no one is suggesting that we return
To the prehistoric notion
Of becoming hunter-gatherers once more

Nature

When you think of nature
Do you think of mountains?
Of valleys, rivers and streams
Of caves, oceans and trees
Perhaps wildlife in natural habitats
Untainted and unpolluted
Yet what is untouched?
Totally au naturel?

The butterfly effect
Where everything affects something
Even if you rolled back the years
Rolled back millions and eons of years
To when there were hunter-gatherers
Even then, was the world really natural?
The fish in waters hunted
Predator animals hunting their prey
Including humans as part of the animal kingdom

And now with emphasis on climate change
Can we really try and be more natural?
Use less carbon emissions?
Could you live without the comfort of your car?
Or public transport?
Never wear make-up
Always be natural
That means no perfumed scents
Including bubble bath and shower gels
No shaving
Not just the beards, men

But no shaving anywhere, men and women
Just natural as other animals

p.s. And this poem
Is just the tip of the iceberg concerning nature
And yes, pun intended
The iceberg being part of the physical world
Part of nature
But also affected by humans
And their impact on the natural world

Nature Reserve

A large piece of land
Preserved for nature
For both fauna and flora
Animals flourishing
Rare flowers and trees existing

Each reserve unique
A sanctuary to try and avoid extinction
Yet there will always be an element
Of survival of the fittest
But with a helping hand supporting all inhabitants

Nature Versus Nurture

It's a debate that has gone on for decades
Whether nature and innate instincts
Have more or less of an impact
On a person's personality and characteristics
Than nurture and the way you are raised
The same debate being applied to different animals

There is an argument that a parent
Can raise their children exactly the same
Showing them the same affection
But they can all turn out differently
Just like their physical attributes can be different

To be humane and humanity
Encompasses the attributes
Of compassion, sympathy and empathy
Those words suggest being benign
An instinct for goodness
Yet that does not explain those who are deemed bad
Sociopaths, psychopaths, liars, corruption and the like

Perhaps we all have a different ratio
Of nature and nurture impact on our personality
Just like we all have different levels
Of oestrogen, hormones and testosterone

Look in the metaphorical mirror
Who or what has influenced you
People
Good and bad experiences

Poverty and affluence
Or have you always felt
That you have always been your own person
Not influenced in the slightest
Never wavering from your ideals

Finally, look in that mirror again
The mirror of truth and revelations
Are you an influencer?
Do you try to coerce or manipulate?
Perhaps gently use persuasive arguments
Are you certain you do not influence?
Never tried to get someone to like you?
To fall in love with you?
Never influenced your work colleagues or managers?
Never suggested your neighbour prune their overhanging
  branches?
What influence do you have on the next generation?
On your children?

Stand in front of that mirror
Close your eyes
Breathe in deep
Exhale
Open your eyes
Who do you see?
Who is the real you?

Nature Versus Nurture:

Round Two

In the one corner
We have nurture:
Your parents
Siblings
Friends and rivals
Neighbours
Your managers
Your work colleagues
Commuters to work
Shoppers in the supermarkets
The internet
Media, including social media

In the other corner
We have nature:
Your soul
Your spirit
Your physique
Oestrogen, hormone and testosterone levels
Your heart
Empathy
Tolerance
Anger

It's going to be a battle extraordinaire
All enter the ring
Wait for the bell

Ding-ding
And they're off

Friends and rivals are fighting amongst themselves
Wow, the punching is fierce
Oh, here comes the supermarket owners
Tempting you with free chocolates
Oh, your hands are reaching out
Naively believing that free means free
Your parents are feigning being frail
Your empathy levels are rising
You're reaching out to the parents
And a kick in the stomach from a sibling
Anger is rising
In tandem with your heart rate
But your soul and spirit remain static, staunch and firm
Ding-ding
End of round one

No one knocked out just yet
All influencers still around
Whispers going on
As new tactics are being discussed
Who will win?
It's nature versus nurture
All still to play for

Naturist

From a linguistics point of view
You might be mistaken to think
That a *naturist* is someone who is
Concerned with nature
Passionate about nature
Increasing their knowledge through learning
Going on hikes in mountains and valleys
Going to archaeological excavations
No

A *naturist* is something completely different
They might have the above-listed interests
But a *naturist* is someone who practises
Non-sexual nudity in private and public
It might be because they want to be closer to nature
In their natural birthday suits like other animals
Or they might just feel more comfortable
Whatever the reason for being a *naturist*
They deserved a poem in this collection

Ocean

You are huge
Engulfing so much space
Awash with your saltiness
Yet also so refreshing

Your healthy colour
Can easily be tainted
Polluted and damaged
Which is what humans do best

You travel with speed
And can also be stoic
Lazy and relaxing
A haven for many

You are a holder of secrets
Dark, deep and hidden
Determined for your mysteries
To remain undiscovered forever

Oxygen

To us mere mortals
It is something we cannot usually see
It is there and essential for us to breathe
For us to live and prosper and be healthy
Not just for us humans
But for plants, animals and even fungi

So no matter how rich you become
It is the things that are free and in abundance
That you really need to survive
Just like years ago for the hunter-gatherers
Yet it is the rich that pollute the most
That is endangering what we need to live

Take a few deep breaths
Inhale and exhale
Feel how precious that is
And perhaps invest a little time
In learning how to give back
How to ensure that oxygen thrives

Ozone Layer

You are there
Surrounding the earth
A layer of protection
From harmful sun rays
Like clingfilm over food
Or wearing a condom
Only with you
You exist naturally
But as with all things
What we humans do
Can dilute you
To the brink of extinction

Pebbles

Over the years we erode
Still maintaining weight
The weight of life;
Memories and regrets
Happiness and tragedies
But through it all
With age we become smaller
Eroded into something almost insignificant
As we are just one of billions
But each one of us has gained invaluable knowledge
Realising the preciousness of life
The shortness of when we were giants
Our souls and spirits have become
Smooth and polished as a pebble

Photosynthesis

You are complex to understand
Able to transform
Metamorphose into something magnificent
Like a flash of light
Enabling us all to breathe
Inhaling your brilliance

Plants

You thrive
Looking vibrant
Amazingly beautiful
Enjoying all types of weather
Yet you are also stoic
A vegetative state
Of no feelings whatsoever

Quarry

You are not natural
You are a parasite
Fuelled by greed

You are an attacker
Of the natural world
Ruthlessly excavating and destroying

Once you've made your millions
You just abandon
Leaving behind a massive hole

Rain

When it rains
We associate that rainfall
With doom and gloom
A dreary and wet day
Taking shelter
And moaning about the rain

Yet it replenishes fresh water
Feeds the thirsty trees and flowers
Creates crisp air which we breathe
Washes down dirty cars and windows
Gives us a break from the sun
Reminding us we are not in control of everything

Rivers

Still water
Like life when caught in a rut
A dull existence of merely living
Or fast flowing
Speed and adventures
With bumps against pebbles and rocks
Debris representing the unwanted aspects
When life is not going according to plans
Cancer and the like causing pain
Then the freshness of the water
Like exhilarating experiences
Precious moments with loved ones
The breeze against the water
Tickling and titillating
Orgasmic pleasure
Then the reflection aspect
Looking at yourself
Do you like what you see?
Are you Narcissus who falls in love
With his own reflection?
Or do you despair
Angry or embarrassed
Disappointed
A mirror of truth
For the rivers can run deep
Hiding your true self in murky depths
Or rising to the surface
Transparent as fresh water

Rocks

The crust of the earth
Hard and rough
Magnificent in stature
Amazing to capture in art
But even the toughest
In the right circumstances
Can crumble and even erode

Salt

Chalk-coloured granules
Extracted from precious salt mines
And salt lakes
Seasoning food to rival Ambrosia;
The food of the Olympian Gods
Becoming delicious and addictive

Yet as the eons have passed
It has almost been forgotten
That salt originated from the sin of one woman
Never named
Merely referred to as Lot's wife

So every time you taste salt
You're becoming devoted
To tasting her disobedience
And her sinful curiosity

Can you feel her?
She's living inside you
Tempting you to naughty desires

You are being swayed
To her wicked ways

It's now part of your DNA

Salt and Pepper

You are an example
That despite differences
Some things and some people
Belong together

You are an example
That black and white
Can blend and create
The most amazing flavours

Sprinkled seasoning
Of salty and hot characters
Is a fusion like no other
Activating and heightening all senses

You have become addictive
Always side by side
Tempting others into your dance
Of white angels and black demons

Seashells

You are beautiful to look at
Beautiful to hold and caress
But do they realise
That you are merely an empty shell

That once you were alive
Soft and delicate
Fragile to the extreme
But nature took its toll

Your death is not even recorded
Nothing left
Like the mass graves in wartime
You are just lying there

No one to even bury you in the sand
Along with so many other victims
Your vibrancy all washed up
For no one lives forever

Seasons

The seasons come and go
Spring with buds blossoming
Crisp fresh air
Followed by summer and the heat
Holidays and excursions
Autumn and the auburn leaves
Falling from trees and getting mushy
It's getting colder
Winter is soon here
Wind and snow and ice
Well that's how it used to be
Ask your parents' and grandparents' generations
Each season was virtually the same as the last
Seldom was there extreme weather
Rare was the cold of winter in the summer
Or autumn weather in winter
Affecting migration of birds
Of bees pollinating flowers
It's not a myth
It's called climate change
It's real and it's here NOW

Snow

You are a reminder
Of just how short
And precious life is

You start out all innocent
White and soft as an angel's feathers
Causing a cold chill in those who see you
Amazed at your beauty
There is laughter
Excitement
Running around
Childish shouting with enthusiasm

But soon you are muddy
Trodden on by mighty and heavy boots
The stomping of those who don't care
Melting you away
Your life ruined
Shrinking

    Until

      Nothing

In other words
Once buried
You are very soon forgotten
No matter how much laughter and excitement
You brought into the lives of others

Sounds

The crashing of waves
Against rough strong rocks
A war over time
That slowly erodes crumbs of rock

Almost silent sounds of hikers
Boots stomping on mud
That splatters in sound and motion
Varied animal sounds in forests

The tranquillity of the sun
Rays silently warming the earth
Administering good and evil
As cells on skin begin to alter

Pitter-patter sounds of rain
Winds that howl and even growl
Soft chills of winter's snow
Sliding ice that causes broken bones

There are so many sounds of nature
Beautiful to watch, but in an instant
Can turn dangerous and ferocious
Just like human animalistic personalities

Stars

Although there are millions and billions of you
Essentially making you very, very common
Each and every one of YOU
Has your own brightness and shine
All of you are stars

Stream

Water flowing
Slow and steady
Or fast and furiously
Clear and refreshing
Or murky and dirty
Just like in life
The ups and downs
We are but a stream
Feeding into the ocean
A fibre amongst many fibres
That together forms clarity
Order over chaos
Perhaps the stream is just a tiny piece
One stroke of a paintbrush
Absorbed into the many strokes
In order to make something substantial
The insignificant flowing in one direction
To create something significant
All those brush strokes
Creating the ultimate masterpiece

Stream

(variant version)

There are streams of water
Flowing gently and calmly
Soothing in sight and sound

There is the streaming
Of movies, music and more
Addicted to watching and listening

Then there are the tears
Of sorrow and happiness
Echoing the silent streams of still water

Study of Nature

There is no single world that encapsulates
The study of nature in its entirety
The natural sciences can include
Astronomy, biology, chemistry,
Earth science and physics
There is the term 'natural history';
The study of living things
But which can also include
Geology, meteorology and palaeontology
Geoscience is an alternative naming of earth science
Then there is climatology, environmental science
Geography, oceanography and the list goes on
So perhaps it's time to create a word
That captures the essence of studying
Anything and everything to do with nature

Sun

You are not just hot
You're the hottest
Instantly recognisable

You're awesome
Men and women alike
Melting in your presence

A star shining bright
Thrusting light in every
Direction that you look at

Swamp

You have a reputation
For being dirty
Drenched and muddy
Dangerous and scary
Pungent and smelly

Yet you should be proud
You're natural
Eco-friendly
Not bothered about
Manufactured beauty

Thunder and Lightning

Working cohesively as a team
Can build spaceships
To fly to Mars and beyond

But not all who work in partnership
Use hard work and creativity
In a benign, constructive way

Just like the thunderbolts of Zeus
Some alliances can cause devastation
As strong as thunder and lightning

Thunderstorm

A shower
Of uncontrollable proportions
Powerful and extreme
Pelting down new oceans

Accompanied by
Frightening lightning shows
And thunderous acoustics
Creating ricocheting rhythms of fear

Ripping and tearing
Through the sky itself
As though the Gods want
A glimpse of the earth

Tricked and trapped eons ago
Perhaps those Ancient Gods
Are trying to escape
Or they're feuding and at war once more

Tidal Waves

Nature can be so beautiful
But there are also elements of nature
That are cruel and brutal
Unrelenting in their viciousness
You encapsulate the very worst
Of what nature can do
Forceful and devastating in your endeavour
Can you imagine what you could achieve
If your enthusiasm was curbed with goodness
Instead of awash with hate and even
Murderous intent?

Tornado

You are violent and brutal
Vicious and savage
Uncontrollable rage
Trying to calm you is futile

You are a whirlwind disaster
Exceptionally destructive
Ultimately catastrophic
You are your own master

There is no rationality
To your hurtful temper
Which we all remember
Whilst wreckful in criminality

You then leave and go elsewhere
Continuing your devastation
Your reprehensible annihilation
Precious things thrown like toys into the air

Unnatural

There is an assumption
That if something is natural
Then that is correct
A logical assumption to then follow
Is that if something is unnatural
Then that must be wrong
Personally, I would disagree

A natural birth can be wonderful
But an unnatural birth might include
Pain relief given during childbirth
Or a caesarean birth
Surely, despite the unnatural nature
Those births are still wondrous
Possibly even miraculous

A biological mother or father
Can be great at parenthood
But they could also be monstrous parents
There are those who abuse and neglect their children
An adoptive parent is not the natural birth parent
But they could be superb at parenting
Or not
In essence, natural does not necessarily mean good

Valley

You have natural depth
That is amazing and beautiful
Yet with anything that is deep
There can be a sorrowful side
Wallowing in mournful moments
So low that your tears become rivers
Uncontrollable and drowning
Hiding your genuine magnificence

Volcano

You are magnificent to look at
Yet completely dangerous
Sizzling beneath the surface
Ready to erupt and explode
When you become active
No one is safe
Full flow magna strength and volatility
Burning everything and everyone in your way
You don't calm down easily
Like an uncontrollable gas explosion
When you do eventually calm down
Temperature still melting hot
It's as though your tantrum
Has become world famous
Preserved for an eternity

Walking

It is an excellent philosophy
To take the time to walk
Go and see nature
It's all around
In parks and treks
Yes there is pollution from cars
But walk amongst the trees
See the flowers
The rivers and streams
Breathe in that air
Experience what nature has to offer
There are so many places
Dedicated conservation areas
Wildlife to see
Not just in zoos
Deer galloping or feeding
And the birds in the gardens
Along with butterflies and bees
Walking at pace is good for your health
Walking slowly to capture new experiences
Well that's so cathartic
You never know
It might even extend your life

Walking

(variant version)

It's a cathartic thing to do
Walk in a park or nature reserve
To where you need to go by foot
Or by wheelchair
Breathe in fresh air
Fill those lungs
Expand them and make them healthy
Smell the roses as the cliché says
The fresh dew on grass and flowers
Dew-drenched and drooling flimsy petals
Breezy winds tickling leaves that giggle
Twigs and branches swaying with belly-aching laughter
Take the time to commute by walking
Contributing to the fresh air
Lessening the pollution and increasing your wealth
But more importantly, investing in your health

Waterfall

You have a very distinctive sound
Husky, powerful and raspy
Rushing with amazing beauty
Mesmerising to watch
Making anyone who views you
Want to bathe with you
Becoming fresh and invigorated

Weather

It's the British thing to do
To discuss the weather
Is it going to be hot or cold?
Wet or dry?
Will it be calm or windy?
Clear or cloudy?

It's everywhere
Before and after the news begins and ends
On your mobile phone
Is the current weather
Predictions for the weather
And did you accessorise with an umbrella or hat

Full English breakfast
Fish and chips
A hot cup of tea
Gossiping
And discussing the weather
Is what identifies your level of Britishness

Whirlpool

Your existence
Is like something from ancient myths
Rare and powerful as Charybdis
Swirling around with rage
Enough to sink ships
And to drown heroes and warriors

Wildfires

Your rage
Is wild and uncontrollable
Erupting out of nowhere
An unplanned event
That burns and scorches
You are intense
Ignited wrath flaring in strength
Determined to leave your mark
Of burnt cinders and ash

Wildlife

They are animals
That are undomesticated
Living in their wild natural habitats
Prey and predators co-existing and surviving

Yet with the expansion of human urbanisation
Excessive greed for illegal trading
Of live and dead animals and their meat, skins, tusks, etc
An extinction in natural habitats and animals is inevitable

Where there is evil, there is also good
Men and women working hard to preserve animal rights
To prevent extinction and illegal trades
Aiding the survival of wildlife

Do you care?
Do you think about the shrinking worlds of wildlife?
Of animals in the sky, land and oceans
Or are you only concerned for your own survival?

Wind

When you are calm
You are like a gentle breeze
Soothing and generating a low chill
Virtually breathing life back
To those whose lives have become mundane
Dull and uneventful

However, there are also times
When your breeze becomes heightened
Gusty energy and speed
Raging and angry
So strong that you could fell trees
Wreaking havoc across the lands

Zoo

No matter how much propaganda
You cannot hide the facts
You're unnatural
You're a kidnapper
A money-hungry entrepreneur
Resulting in me questioning
Who the real animals are in a zoo

Epilogue

The following poem was originally published in *Animal in YOU?* It seemed appropriate to include it in this volume as well.

King of the Jungles and the Oceans

They say that the lion is the King of the Jungle
There are Kings and Queens of countries
Mythical Gods of the Earth and of the oceans
But there is only one real King
Of sea and of land
Educating the masses for decades
Showcasing mammals, anthropoids, birds
Amphibians, Reptiles, Vertebrae, etc
Through innovative documentaries
Braving the wild forests,
Polar regions and depths of the ocean
Award-winning
Even having flora and fauna named after him
Revealing truths about the dangers of extinction
Of individual species and of the planet
The distinctive voice of knowledge and education
In awe of the King of the Planet
Sir David Attenborough

Other books by Mario Panayi

1 Birth Life Burial

2 Myths and Make-Believe

3 Do You Recognise Yourself?

4 Animal in You?

5 Glimpses of Epic Greek Myths

6 What Drink Are You?

7 Political Perspectives

8 Selections 2021/2022 Edition

9 What Cake or Dessert Are YOU?

10 What Flower, Bush or Tree are YOU?

11 What Fruit Are YOU?

12 Worst Cook Book EVER

13 Book 13: Luck

14 Everything butt the Kitchen Sink

15 Clothes and Friends